IRELAND'S HOLY PLACES

The most popular place of pilgrimage in Ireland today is Knock, a village in County Mayo where, in 1879, fifteen villagers claimed to have seen a vision of the Virgin Mary with St John and St Joseph. A million people visit Knock every year, and about 600 cures have been attributed to the intercession of the Virgin at this site. Ireland is full of places of religious importance. Benedictines, Augustinians, Franciscans, Dominicans and Cistercians all had numerous communities in Ireland, and though many of their monasteries are now in ruins they remain as places where people go to find God and to pray.

By the same author:

Ulster & Its Future After the Troubles (1977)
Ulster & The German Solution (1978)
Ulster & The British Connection (1979)
Ulster & The Lords of the North (1980)
Ulster & The Middle Ages (1982)
Ulster & St Patrick (1984)
The Twilight Pagans (1990)
Enemy of England (1991)
The Great Siege (2002)
Ulster in the Age of Saint Comgall of Bangor (2004)
Ulster Blood (2005)
King William's Victory (2006)
Ulster Stock (2007)
Famine in the Land of Ulster (2008)
Pre-Christian Ulster (2009)
The Glens of Antrim (2010)
Ulster Women – A Short History (2010)
The Invasion of Ulster (2010)
Ulster in the Viking Age (2011)
Ulster in the Eighteenth Century (2011)
Ulster in the History of Ireland (2012)
Rathlin Island (2013)
Saint Patrick's Missionary Journeys in Ireland (2015)
The Story of Carrickfergus (2015)

IRELAND'S HOLY PLACES

Michael Sheane

ARTHUR H. STOCKWELL LTD
Torrs Park, Ilfracombe, Devon, EX34 8BA
Established 1898
www.ahstockwell.co.uk

British Library Cataloguing-in-Publication Data.
A catalogue record for this book is available
from the British Library.

ISBN 978-0-7223-4665-5
Printed in Great Britain by
Arthur H. Stockwell Ltd
Torrs Park Ilfracombe
Devon EX34 8BA

CONTENTS

THE AGE OF REFORM AND AFTER

The decline of the ancient monastic ideal and the onset of laxity and corruption cannot be easily dated, but it may be pointed out that by the late tenth century the Church in Ireland was in a sorry state. But the conditions of the Church in Europe was in many ways even worse: the state of the Church posed difficult questions for the reformers. Many problems faced the Church at that time. The collapse of the great empire that the emperor Charlemagne had founded in 885 saw Europe disintegrate into many feudal states. For two centuries the papacy degenerated. The cancer was not confined to Rome, for abuses were widespread. Often bishoprics and abbacies were auctioned to the highest bidder. Priests could marry and pass on to their sons the pickings they had accumulated in the ecclesiastical rat race. Deprived of sound leadership the religion of the laity had declined into ignorance and superstition.

The Irish Church and society were in a state of disarray in the middle of the eleventh century. The raids of the Vikings had taken their toll. Irish society was divided into a patchwork of kingdoms, or *tuatha*. The Vikings, however, were defeated at the Battle of Clontarf in 1014.

A serious vacuum was created within the Church by the decline of the old monastic orders. Though there was a multitude of bishops, there was not a diocesan structure; the monks roamed the countryside doing duty on a freelance basis. Many abbeys were mere chattles of the ruling families. No wonder when Pope Gregory VII first addressed the Irish people, perhaps sometime in the mid 1070s, he did so not through bishops or abbots, but through the Kings of Munster. Gregory told Turlough, King of Munster, to appeal directly to Rome should any problems occur which required the Pope's help. He urged the Irish bishops and abbots to remember their duty of loyalty to the Holy See.

It is fashionable these days to dismiss canonists as ecclesiastical pedants. The Pope had good reason to be worried about the state of Ireland: the laity were neglected; marriage customs were often the cause of scandal. Abbeys were often the personal fiefs of individual families, which made reform almost impossible to achieve. Some determined souls attempted to reform the monasteries on the basis of the old Irish ideal.

Columba's beloved monastery at Derry, or Doire, and a more modern one at Tallaght, near Dublin, were outstanding examples of what could be achieved given favourable circumstances. The future lay elsewhere: within a century Ireland would be dotted with religious orders bearing strange-looking names, and there would be a diocesan structure throughout the country that would revolutionize the style and direction of the Irish Church. The most urgent reform was to establish dioceses. The first steps in setting up a diocesan structure for the whole island were taken in 1101 at a council in Cashel, seat of the Kings of Munster. The council, including chiefs and bishops, was presided over by King Murtagh O'Brien. It laid the ground for major reforms in the structure of Church government that were carried forward by the

Council of Rathbreasail in 1111 and completed by the Synod of Kells/Mellifont in 1152.

But the Council of Cashel is chiefly noted for a remarkable gesture: King Murtagh had handed over the Rock of Cashel to the Church, a remarkable limestone outcrop which rises 200 feet from the plains of Tipperary. The great rock had been in the hands of the Munster kings for over 730 years and the great Brian Boru had been crowned there. But there is reason to believe that Murtagh's gift was not entirely disinterested. Nevertheless he was to make Cashel one of the leading ecclesiastical centres of Ireland, second only to Armagh.

Ten years later the reformers received a boost when Cashel became one of its two Irish archbishoprics and Malchus became its first archbishop; he ended his days as Bishop of Waterford. The Council of Cashel is also noted for outlawing simony, which was rampant in the Church so subject to secular power. Cashel had initiated the process of reform, but it could get nowhere without the leadership of Armagh, the chief ecclesiastical centre, which perhaps did not play a part in the first council. Five years after the Council of Cashel, Armagh got a new archbishop who was to begin a new era for the city of St Patrick. He was Celsus, latest in a line of coarbs or heirs to the abbacy of Armagh from the Clann Sinaich. The choice of abbots by right of inheritance was according to Gaelic law, but unless it was ended, or at least moderated, the prospects of reform were not bright. The break with a 200-year-old tradition came with Celsus, who was converted to reform, and he became a priest and a bishop. But there would still be problems to be solved, including an obdurate heir who fled Armagh with the Staff of Jesus and the Book of Armagh, symbols of office – the decision of Celsus to opt for reform was sufficient to sway the issue eventually.

THE MOVING SPIRIT

When Celsus assumed office at Armagh, the city's famous school had a clever twelve-year-old pupil under the care of an ascetic, Imar O'Hagan. The boy was Malachy, born in Armagh, the son of a teacher at the school. Even then he had a reputation for piety and a bent for monastic life. He was ordained by Celsus in 1119. Soon afterwards, Bishop Samuel of Dublin died and Celsus was called to assume temporary responsibility for the vacant see of Armagh in his absence. Without much hesitation and with great courage Celsus chose the twenty-five-year-old priest as his vicar.

Only eight years before, in 1111, the Council of Rathbreasail had set up the first diocesan structure in Ireland. The country was divided into two provinces, Cashel in the south and Armagh in the north, with twelve suffragan dioceses in each.

To assume responsibility for what was the main diocese at twenty-five was demanding much of Malachy, but he was up to the task. Not content with merely administering the system, he set up in a chain a whole series of changes in line with the Gregorian reform. We learn much about Malachy from his great contemporary St Bernard of Clairvaux, who was four years his senior. That Bernard thought much of him is clear from the *Life of St Malachy*, which he wrote after Malachy's death in 1148. St Bernard, like many hagiographers before and after him, found it necessary to paint everything in terms of black and white, without intermediate shades of grey, the better to highlight Malachy's virtues.

Starting from a self-reforming base, the young Malachy introduced into Armagh a revitalized monastic life. He urged confession upon the people. He brought back the sacrament of confirmation, which had fallen into abeyance, and revised the marriage contract along Christian lines.

Malachy was always drawn to the monastic life. Throughout his active life he frequently returned to the enclosure to refresh his spirit. He was so impressed by the faithfulness and austerity with which the monks of Clairvaux lived that he wished to join the monastery and end his days there. He petitioned the Pope to this effect, but permission was refused. The Pope had other work for the saint. After his spell as vicar of Armagh came to an end Malachy went south to spend two years with the saintly Malchus in the monastery of Lismore, famous for its peace and quiet. One of the members of the Lismore community was Cormac MacCarthy, who had sought refuge there after being exiled by his brother Donagh. Cormac was later to become King-Bishop of Cashel and to build Cormac's Chapel on the Rock. The friendship forged between Malachy and Cormac at Lismore was to be of immense value in the years to come.

Malachy returned north to become abbot of St Comgall's old monastery at Bangor, which had long since lost its lustre. Then in 1124 he became Bishop of Connor. St Bernard has much to say of this period because Malachy experienced serious harassment, including a violent raid on Bangor from the local chief opposed to reform. The chief wanted Malachy to flee to Lismore. The differences between Malachy and the chief must have been serious to have ended in such an act of violence.

From Lismore, Malachy set out with a group of followers to found a monastic settlement at an unknown site, widely believed to have been in County Kerry. But Celsus died in 1129, leaving the Armagh see open to Malachy. Malachy was loath to take up the see, but the papal legate thought that he should obey the Pope. So back Malachy went to his native city, to be met by the reopening of the old dispute about the coarbship of heirs of Armagh. The coarbs of Armagh were educated men, but usually married and not priests. Their reluctance to give in to the reformers' demands for an end to hereditary rights was due to the immense prestige Armagh enjoyed as the city of St Patrick.

Celsus had broken with tradition by becoming a priest. He was the fourth in a line of descendants stretching back to his great-great-grandfather to have held the office. The struggle for the coarbship after Celsus's death is complicated, but it need not concern us here. Malachy, with the help of reformers, triumphed in the end.

In 1137 he won the main battle for reform. Malachy resigned as a gesture for peace. He was succeeded by St Gelasius, abbot of the reformed monastery of Derry, or Doire. Malachy's act was a brave one, but it did not help to heal the wounds and caused little damage to the Church in Ireland. Still only forty-three, Malachy enjoyed much prestige and was acknowledged to be the leader of the Church in Ireland though he no longer held the Armagh see. He became Bishop of Down and he again set about this reforming work at Bangor, which had been interrupted a few years before by the hostile chief. But his horizons were wider than Down, and in 1139 he went to Rome to obtain the Pope's approval for the reforming programme in the island. It was on his way to Rome that in 1140 he called at Clairvaux and first met St Bernard.

The meeting had important consequences for the Church in Ireland. Bernard was a nobleman, the third of seven children, six of whom were boys. He was born in a village near Dijon in 1090 and educated at a school of secular canons. He was attached to his mother, and when she died he was a youth of seventeen, uncertain of his future. Malachy is known to have visited the great Augustinian abbey at Arrouaise, near Arras, after his visit to Clairvaux, and to have been struck by the suitability of their rule to the Irish situation. In many ways the members of the old monastic establishments in Ireland resembled regular canons rather than monks. Their monasteries served as cathedrals and parish churches, and the priests ministered to the lay folk in much the same way as the secular clergy do today.

St Malachy influenced the spread of the canons in Ireland, particularly in the north, but that he introduced them is more open to doubt. It is not unlikely that the first foundation of the canons was in his diocese at Lough Derg in 1134 when Malachy was Archbishop of Armagh, and also four years later, he was at Downpatrick when he was Bishop of Down. But the Augustinian canons were so widespread in Ireland in such a short time (there were sixty-two houses at the time of the Norman invasion) that it would be unwise to attribute it to any single source or any single pattern. Their arrival predates that of the Cistercians by seven years.

It is likely that Malachy was responsible for the introduction of another order into Ireland – the Benedictine monks of the Savignac congregation. This was an order founded in 1105 by a French canon, St Vitalis, to be a rule of primitive Benedictine strictness. It was part of the period of widespread reform that also gave birth to the Cistercians. Their first house in Ireland was at Erenagh, County Down, almost certainly sponsored by Malachy. The order opened another house in Dublin, in 1139. Both houses joined the Cistercians in 1147.

These achievements were remarkable byproducts of Malachy's main mission at this time, to secure papal approval for the reform programme, and to get Pope Innocent II to grant palls – symbols of the archiepiscopal office – to Armagh and Cashel. Innocent gave his approval, but he refused to grant the palls until a more formal request had been tendered. The palls were withheld until the second Synod of Kells/Mellifont, in 1152, when not two but four were granted – to Armagh, Cashel, Dublin and Tuam – and a diocesan structure was established that lasted until the present day, with few changes.

Malachy returned from Rome as papal legate – an office that was much more important than it is today, when it is largely ceremonial. The holder was then literally the representative of the Holy See. Armed with this authority Malachy resumed his efforts for reform, culminating in 1148 with an assembly of 200 bishops and priests on St Patrick's Island, off the coast of County Dublin. It was the first such meeting without the presence of the Irish king. Its aim was to lay the ground rules for the discipline of the clergy and laity. The meeting also decided officially to petition the Pope for the palls. Malachy was asked to take the petition to Rome, but, worn out by ill-health, he was loath to go. But he was persuaded after it was pointed out to him that he had become friendly with the new Pope, Eugenius III, when he was a monk at Clairvaux during Malachy's visit there. So off Malachy travelled again.

But Malachy was never to see Rome again. The English king, Stephen, caused trouble by refusing to let Malachy embark from England. He had to endure a hazardous boat journey from Scotland to France. He called at Clairvaux, and only just missed the Pope, who had left the monastery a short time before for Italy. Malachy had the company of St Bernard for two weeks, but he became suddenly ill and died. He was buried in front of the high altar.

The years of Malachy's ascendancy were the high watermark of the reform movement. He helped to set the tone for what followed after his death. He did not do so alone; he had many supporters, not least among the laity, for without their support in granting land, endowments and gifts, religious houses would not have become established. In promoting diocesan reform, Malachy had support from both within and outside Ireland, not least from the Popes. The movement continued after his death: in 1152 the great Synod of Kells/Mellifont approved the new diocesan structure with four archdioceses, one each in Leinster, Munster, Ulster and Connaught, with Armagh as the primatial see. Malachy's drive to promote the new religious orders in Ireland also maintained its momentum after his death.

From Mellifont monks travelled forth to found monasteries at Baltinglass, County Wicklow, and Monasteranenagh, County Limerick (1148); Kilbeggan, County Westmeath (1150); Newry, County Down (1153); and Boyle, County Roscommon (1161). In addition the monastery at Monasteranenagh founded Abbeydorney, County Kerry, in 1154.

Two other Cistercian houses soon followed – Jerpoint, County Kilkenny, in 1165, and Holycross, County Tipperary, four years later. Before the Norman invasion of Ireland there were fifteen Cistercian houses.

The Augustinians were even more widespread, though not all their foundations belonged to the same congregation. Most were subject to Arrouaise, except Munster. The great St Laurence O'Toole, a member of the Leinster royal house, an abbot of St Kevin's old house at Glendalough – a monk after Malachy's own heart – extended the Augustinian influence in eastern Ireland after he had become Archbishop of Dublin in 1162. The same year he had persuaded the secular canons of Christ Church Cathedral, Dublin, to adopt the Augustinian rule. Four years later his kinsman, Dermot MacMurrough (the king that requested Norman help in Ireland), installed the Augustinians at All Saints Priory in Dublin.

The earliest foundations of Augustinian canons were at Lough Derg in 1134 and Downpatrick four years later. By 1140 there were Augustinian houses at Duleek, County Meath; Dungiven, County Derry; Elphin, County Roscommon; Kells Abbey, County Antrim; Monaincha Priory, Toomyvara and Roscrea, all in County Tipperary; St Patrick's Island, County Dublin; Saul, County Down; Trim, County Meath; and Tuam, County Galway. By the time of the Norman invasion of Ireland there were also twenty-two houses of Augustinian canonesses, a number of which were double monasteries.

There were two Benedictine houses before the invasion; the most interesting one was at Cashel. This foundation stemmed from a Gaelic monastery at Ratisbon, Germany. The abbot there sent four monks to help the foundation of a house dedicated to St James at Cashel. They included two German tradesmen, one a carpenter. They played a large part in the building of Cormac's Chapel, giving it a Teutonic flavour uncommon in Irish church architecture. It is almost certain that the chapel was built for the Benedictines. There was another Benedictine house at Rosscarbery, County Cork, founded in 1148 by an Irish monk from Würzburg, Germany, who had become Bishop of Ross. The Cluniac monks had one foundation, at Athlone Priory, said to have been founded in 1150 by Turlough O'Connor, King of Connaught, who was a notable medieval lay benefactor. He also founded Cong Abbey, County Mayo, for the Augustinian canons.

THE NORMAN INVASION OF IRELAND AND AFTER

Amid all of this activity, in 1155 a seed was sown in Rome that was to change the course of Irish History. Pope Adrian IV, the only Englishman to have been Pope, granted Ireland to his kinsman King Henry II, to be held by him in 'hereditary right'. This is the famous 'Laudabiliter', the authenticity of which scholars have argued about for centuries. The important thing is that it seems to have been regarded as genuine at the time. It was to provide Henry with the moral authority he required to justify his assumption of power in the island. It could have been that the Pope was obliging the King with an excuse for expansion. It also has been believed that only under the English king could a momentum for reform be maintained in Ireland; the fact is that we do not know.

What is certain is that nobody in the twelfth century would have regarded the Pope as exceeding his authority by such a grant. The ancient Donation of Constantine, by which all islands were said to belong to the Church of Rome, would have justified it. What is puzzling is why Adrian should have regarded Ireland as in need of Norman protection. After all, the reform movement in Ireland was mainly galvanized from within; Rome had enough confidence in the Gaels to appoint four successive papal legates – Gilbert of Limerick, Malachy, Laurence O'Toole and the Cistercian Christian, first abbot of Mellifont. In his petition to the Pope through Adrian's friend John of Salisbury, the philosopher, King Henry pleaded the love of faith and religion as his motive for wanting Ireland, and the Pope seems to have swallowed it.

The Normans came to Ireland in 1169 for reasons that had nothing to do with the love of faith and religion. When they became established they continued the policy of the Gaels by opening up new religious houses in the colonized areas. Most of these were founded from Britain – for example, in 1100 the Earl of Pembroke brought Cistercians from Tintern Abbey, Monmouthshire, to open a new monastery near Duncannon, County Wexford,which they also called Tintern.

In the same year Cistercians from Wales founded a house at Downpatrick. Three houses of the Augustinian canons which opened at Kilkenny between 1193 and 1211 stemmed from Bodmin, Cornwall. Many other Cistercian and Augustinian houses were founded in native areas by well-established monasteries. At the time of the dissolution of the monasteries there were about 120 Augustinian houses and fifty Cistercian abbeys in Ireland.

The Normans also introduced new congregations. Among them were the Premonstratensian canons, also known as the Norbertines and jokingly as the Monstrous Pretensions because of their tongue-twisting name. They were founded by St Norbert in France in 1120. He based the rule on St Augustine's; he was also influenced by Cistercian austerity through Norbert's friendship with St Bernard of Clairvaux. They were introduced into the island from Scotland by John de Courcy, who had also founded Carrickfergus Priory for them in 1183. They eventually opened twelve houses, the last of which (at

Lough Oughter, Trinity Island, County Cavan) closed down sometime in the seventeenth century.

The Holy Cross Fathers, were a congregation of uncertain origin; they were hospitallers, and they were largely confined to the Norman east. They opened their first house at Dundalk in 1189 and eventually had eighteen, several of which (Dublin and Dundalk, for example) also had nuns working in the hospitals.

There were the Knights Templar, an international military order also known as the Poor Knights of Christ, founded in 1118 after the capture of Jerusalem by Godfrey de Bouillon, a French noble. The influence of St Bernard was obvious in their early rule, but they grew in wealth and they were eventually suppressed by Rome in 1312. They had come to Ireland in 1180 when they founded houses at Crook, County Waterford, and Clontarf, Dublin, eventually opening fifteen houses, but their houses passed to the Knights Hospitaller on suppression.

The Knights Hospitaller, another international order of uncertain origin, became known in the eleventh century as the Knights of the Order of the Hospital of St John of Jerusalem because their headquarters were at a hospital in the region dedicated to St John the Baptist. They had originally provided hospitality for pilgrims and care of the sick. They acquired a strong military base in Ireland, and were often used as a military and police force by the Normans. Many of them had accompanied the invasion of the country for this purpose. They had a headquarters at Kilmainham, Dublin, founded in 1174, from where the prior ruled twenty-one houses, mostly in the Irish colony. According to a Father Gwynn and Neville Hadcock, there were only a handful of hospitallers in Ireland at the time of the dissolution; most of their houses had been farmed out.

With such an explosion of religious houses, founded on a wave of religious and political fervour, it was not surprising that there were lapses from the high ideals of the founders. Several of the Cistercian houses rebelled against the authority of the mother house at Cîteaux and they were only brought to heel with much trouble in the face of threats to life and limb. Following the first wave of new orders and congregations of monks, canons, brothers and nuns came the second equally strong influx of the newly founded friars – Dominicans, Franciscans and Carmelites.

The friars were a new departure in religious tradition. Lacking corporate possessions, they engaged in direct teaching to the faithful, and above all they were mobile; unlike the monks or canons they were not confined to one settlement.

They came to Ireland initially from Britain, but unlike previous Norman foundations they did not confine themselves to the colonized lands. The Dominicans arrived first, founding houses in Dublin and Drogheda in 1124. New foundations followed in Waterford (1226), Limerick (1227), Cork (1229), Mullingar (1237), Athenry, County Galway (1241), Cashel and Tralee (1243) and Coleraine and Newtownards (1244). Eleven new foundations were to follow up to the first great influx of Dominicans at the beginning of the fourteenth century – Sligo, Roscommon, Athy, Trim, Arklow, Youghal, Lorrha, Derry, Kilmallock and Carlingford.

The Franciscans arrived in 1229 and opened their first house at Youghal; the following year another followed at Kilkenny, then Carrickfergus (1232), Dublin (1233), Multyfarnham (1236), Athlone (1239), Timoleague, Downpatrick, Waterford and Drogheda (1240), Castledermot (1247), Dundalk (1248), New Ross and

Claregalway (1250), Nenagh (1252), Ardfert (1253), Kildare (1254), Armagh (1263), Cashel (1265), Limerick (1267), Wexford and Wicklow (1268), Clonmel (1269), Buttevant (1276), Trim (1282), Killeigh (1283), Galway (l296), Cavan (1325) and Carrickbeg (1336).

The Carmelites were late arrivals, starting their foundation in l272, and in Dublin two years later. They were under the stern leadership of St Simon Stock, the English-born general. They eventually opened fifteen houses in Ireland. They had important foundations at Loughrea, Galway and Kinsale.

The last of the friars to arrive were the Augustinians, a mendicant branch of the original canons. They opened their first house in Dublin in 1282 and their second at Dungarvan, County Waterford, eight years later. New foundations followed the next year at Drogheda and Tipperary. The last, and eleventh, a mendicant foundation, was at New Ross in 1320.

The friars stimulated religious life in the country. They lived close to the people and were attentive to their spiritual needs. They complemented each other – Dominicans were essentially preachers; the Franciscans were Christian social workers; and both the Carmelites and the Augustinian friars were influenced by, though not absorbed by, the Dominicans.

Within a short time the Dominicans and Franciscans were supplying bishops to Irish sees, as the Cistercians had done before.

But there were eventually serious problems caused by the clash of cultures. The gradual dominance of England in the Gaelic Church formed a channel for the energies, feelings and thinking of an alien culture and language. It was confined to the planted areas of the east, eventually channelling the energies of religious people away from their essential function long before the Reformation. In the Middle Ages there was a dislocation between the political and the religious, though trouble in one affected the other.

There was also the disaster of the Black Death, a deadly plague that brought devastation to the whole of Christendom. In the summer of 1349 the Archbishop of Armagh told the Pope at Avignon that the Black Death had killed two-thirds of the population of England, but had left Ireland relatively alone. But he was misinformed – the dreaded plague brought disaster to Ireland. Fourteen thousand people died in Dublin alone between the beginning of August and Christmas 1348 – so reported the Franciscan John Clyn, who noted that twenty-five friars had died in the house at Drogheda and twenty-three in Dublin. There is reason to believe that John Clyn may have exaggerated his estimate, but nevertheless the toll taken by the Black Death was quite great and must have reduced and weakened the population of the religious.

THE NORMAN HERITAGE

The Irish countryside is well endowed with the remains of medieval monasteries and religious houses, but most of them are in ruins. Some have been incorporated into new buildings erected in the Stuart and Georgian eras by the Church of Ireland. Some are more than ruins.

Ballintubber Abbey, County Mayo, for example, is the only church in the British Isles where Mass has been said continually for over 750 years. It was founded in 1216 by Cathal O'Conor, King of Connaught, for the Augustinian canons. It survived much – a fire in 1263, the dissolution and a violent visit by Cromwell's men. Mainly due to the efforts of a local priest, Father T. A. Egan, the ruined parts of the abbey were attended to in the early 1960s and it was completed in 1964, though a part of the building had been used as a Catholic chapel for many years. The doorway is a good example of the pointed receding arch supported on each side by columns.

Another medieval abbey which has recently been restored is Holycross, County Tipperary, a famous place of pilgrimage in the Middle Ages due to the particle of the true Cross given by Pope Paschal I to King Murtagh O'Brien. It passed through many hands after that until 1909, when it was given into the care of the Ursuline nuns. It is now at their convent in Blackrock, Cork city. Holycross has been restored several times and there is now little trace of the original Romanesque. It has a fine square tower supported by four pointed arches, aisles, transept and side chapels. There are beautiful window traces, seen at their best in the east window, which has six lights for the chancel. There are also the remains of the cloisters, chapter house, abbot's quarters and other buildings.

Another abbey, still partly in use, is Duiske in County Kilkenny. It was founded in 1203 by William Marshall, Earl of Pembroke, who also brought the Cistercians to Tintern, County Wexford, and the Dominicans to Kilkenny city. Duiske was an important abbey with extensive grounds, but its great tower collapsed in 1774. Part of the building was roofed over in 1813 and it is still used as a Roman Catholic church.

The tradition of the true Cross, mentioned in relation to Holycross, recurs in one of Ireland's famous treasures, the Cross of Cong, now in the National Museum in Dublin. It was made in Roscommon in 1223 by order of Turlough O'Connor to enshrine another portion of the Cross. It is on oak with copper plating and Celtic embellishments of gold. It was originally deposited in Tuam Cathedral, but it was taken to Cong by Turlough's son Roderick for safekeeping by the Augustinian canons of the abbey. Here Roderick spent the last fifteen years of his life. The abbey of Cong flourished until the dissolution, but it fell into decay after that; it is now a striking ruin.

The Cistercians' first monastery in Ireland at Mellifont is also in ruins. There are the remains of the gatehouse, a massive structure fifty feet high. Of the abbey church little remains, though clearly it was huge. There are some clustered columns, and a well-preserved doorway in the north wall. The Norman chapter house also survives, two storeys with a beautiful doorway. The most striking survival at Mellifont is the 'Lavabo', an octagonal structure with only four walls remaining, each resting on a fine arch. Above the roof, now missing, was a reservoir which supplied the entire monastery with water. At the northern end of Mellifont village is New Mellifont, a Cistercian house which was established here in 1939 – the first Cistercians at Mellifont since the monastery was dissolved in 1540.

Jerpoint Abbey, County Kilkenny, is a pre-Norman foundation which still has its Irish Romanesque chancel and transepts. The original barrel-vaulted stone roof of the chancel is also preserved. The square central tower is of the fifteenth century. There are several interesting tombs at Jerpoint, including that of the first abbot, who died in 1202. There is also a fine effigy of him (Felix O'Dullany), holding a crozier being gnawed by a snake.

Kilcooley Abbey, in the Slieveardagh Hills of County Tipperary, is a daughter house of Jerpoint, founded by King Donagh O'Brien in 1200. The abbey church and other monastic buildings have interesting features. The chancel and the transepts are very well preserved. The east end of the church is a fifteenth-century restoration of the original. There are some fine carvings over the Gothic door.

Bective Abbey was one of the most important houses of the Cistercians; it lies five miles from Navan, County Meath, with many ruins, mainly of the cloisters.

At Manister, near Croom, County Limerick, are the ruins of Monasterenanagh Abbey, with its chapter house, abbey mill and some extensive carvings.

The ruins of Dunbrody Abbey near the village of Campile, County Wexford, are among the finest in Ireland. The land was originally given to the monks from

Shropshire shortly after the Norman invasion, but it was handed over to St Mary's Abbey, Dublin. Dunbrody Abbey was built in 1182. There is a large church 200 feet long by 140 feet wide at the transepts, with a striking east window and a beautiful west door, heavily ornamented.

Moore Abbey, near Monasterevin, County Kildare, is a large mansion built on the site of an old Cistercian abbey. It was for six years the home of the singer John McCormack.

The ruins of the Cistercian abbey at Boyle, County Roscommon, are a delight, covered in ivy and well preserved. There is a central tower and the usual cruciform church, with domestic quarters, including a kitchen.

Perhaps the most beautifully situated Cistercian abbey was at Inch, three miles from Downpatrick, founded by John de Courcy to atone for his destruction of what was perhaps the first medieval monastery in Ireland – the Benedictine abbey at Erenagh. Inch Abbey lies beside the River Quoile. There is not much left of it except an east window and parts of pillars.

Cashel, with its cathedral and Cormac's Chapel, is perhaps the most important medieval ruin in the country. The chapel is very well preserved. The ruined cathedral is a cruciform structure. The Rock of Cashel is well gifted with relics from the past. The impact is truly dramatic. It is an extraordinary chunk of rock twisted by nature and by man into an awesome sight. It is best seen by standing back from the rock and viewing it in silhouette.

Fore Abbey in County Westmeath is a good example of where a medieval monastery superseded an old Irish one. There was a thriving Celtic settlement there that was founded in 630 by St Fechin. At its peak it is thought that it housed 3,000 monks. But the monastery was repeatedly destroyed by fire from the death of Fechin in 635 until

1170, when it was abandoned. In 1209 Walter de Lacy founded a monastery here, dedicated to St Fechin, for the Benedictines from Évreux in Normandy; there are still many remains of the old foundation. The Benedictine abbey has been restored several times; it is in quite good condition. Its main feature is the cloistered arcade. Despite the proliferation of medieval Augustinian abbeys, there are fewer remains than there are of the Cistercian abbeys.

Ferns has the ruins of an abbey that was burned down in 1154 and rebuilt in 1160 by Dermot MacMurrough, who died there in 1171. There is a tower, the north side wall of the church and priests' rooms.

At Wexford, two miles distant, the Protestant church of St Selskar is on the site of the old abbey choir, and there are the ruins of the abbey near Westgate Tower.

Duleek, County Meath, a noted ecclesiastical centre, has a few remains of two Augustinian abbeys.

There is a partly restored abbey at Pallas, County Longford, and the beautiful ruins of another in the banks of the Moy at Tubbercurry, County Sligo.

One of the most interesting Augustinian ruins is at Adare, County Limerick. There is a square tower, a nave and part of the conventual choir, restored in the last century by the Earls of Dunraven. The cloisters were converted in 1826 into a mausoleum for the Dunraven family.

The oldest Augustinian ruins seem to be the west gable surmounting the belfry of a priory built in about 1101, which forms part of the Protestant parish church at Roscrea, County Tipperary.

At Abbeyside, Dungarvan, the square tower of the thirteenth century priory is now used as the belfry of the adjoining Catholic church.

Other notable Augustinian ruins are at Trim, County Meath; Golden, Cashel and Lorrha, all in County Tipperary;

Ballinasloe, County Galway; Lecanvey, County Mayo; and Dungiven, County Londonderry.

The Franciscans, Dominicans and Carmelites were all orders whose mission was to the people and it is natural that there are numerous remains of their medieval foundations in the towns. In some places the orders are still to be found where their pioneers first put down roots 600–700 years ago. The Franciscan church in John Street, Wexford, is on the site of a priory opened in 1230. The Dominican church in Kilkenny has a tower and some fourteenth-century windows of the famous Black Abbey built in 1225.

The well-preserved Franciscan church off the quay at Waterford has an interesting history. It was richly endowed by King Henry II. But it fell into disuse for nearly a century after the suppression of the monasteries. However, it was revived towards the end of seventeenth century as a chapel for a colony of Huguenot refugees, who retained it until 1819 when it was at last abandoned.

The Franciscans have been associated with Multyfarnham, County Westmeath, for over 600 years. The modern college run by the order is on the site of an old foundation, though the tower of the church is a sixteenth-century structure.

The Norse town of Sligo has notable remains of a thirteenth-century Dominican abbey. The cloisters are in a good state of preservation. There a magnificent east window with exquisite tracery work. The central tower is complete except for the battlements. There is a spacious nave supported by ranges of pillars.

The most striking early Carmelite remains are in Ardee, County Louth, where St Mary's Church of Ireland embraces a portion of the ancient friary, burned down in 1315 by Robert the Bruce. It was later rebuilt, but without a north aisle. Among the features of the old church uncovered is a staircase built into the wall, which has been taken to be the ascent to a pulpit.

Castledermot, County Laois, has many remains of a Franciscan foundation, along with a church dedicated to St Mary. On the north side is a high pointed arch leading to the chapel of the Virgin Mary, with some fine glass windows.

One of the finest ruins is the fifteenth-century friary of Adare, County Limerick. The earliest parts of the ruins are the transept and belfry; the chapels, the dormitory and the infirmary are sixteenth-century additions.

Also at Adare are the remains of the only Trinitarian church in Ireland. It was founded in the thirteenth century for the Order of Redemption of Christ. This order was started in France in 1213 to obtain the release of Christians held in Moslem lands.

The fifteenth-century friary at Askeaton, County Limerick, was used as a Catholic church until 1851. It was built by the 7th Earl of Desmond. The most interesting feature is the grey marble used to build it; this was found in abundance in the region.

Muckross Abbey, now included in the national park at Muckross, near Killarney, is a Franciscan friary, founded by Donal McCarthy in 1488, but some historians think that it was on the site of an earlier friary. The ruins are among the most splendid in Ireland. A large tower separates the nave and the adjoining transept. There are fine cloisters with twenty-two arches in a mixture of Gothic and Irish Romanesque.

The introduction of the diocesan system into Ireland meant the building of cathedrals. Monasteries are essentially rural; but some crown the city. The original cathedrals in Ireland passed out of Roman Catholic hands after the Reformation; they are now, for the most part, the centre of the Church of Ireland dioceses. This partly explains the peculiar anomaly of Dublin, which had two Protestant cathedrals but no Catholic one.

The present Christ Church and St Patrick's cathedrals are both nineteenth-century restorations. It is said that one Donatus built Christ Church in 1138. Strongbow later replaced this with a more elaborate structure. Most of the present cathedral dates from the 1870s. St Patrick's was first built in 1190 and extensively rebuilt in 1390. In the nineteenth century it was saved from ruin by a member of the Guinness family, who put up money to have it restored. Cromwell's men inflicted indignity on St Patrick's Cathedral by using it as a stable for their horses.

St Canice's Cathedral, Kilkenny, suffered a similar fate. There Cromwell's soldiers destroyed windows, doors and monuments, tore off the roof and left the building almost derelict. But the austere and spacious cruciform church still retains its essential features and it is now the cathedral of the Church of Ireland diocese of Ossory.

Limerick Cathedral, dedicated to the Virgin Mary, was opened for worship in 1194. It now houses St Mary's Church and Palace. There are other cathedrals at Leighlinbridge in County Kildare, Tuam, Cavan, Downpatrick and Dromore.

Waterford's Church of Ireland cathedral is on the site of the original Christ Church built by Malchus.

The Church of Ireland cathedral at Armagh is believed to occupy the site of a church built by the great St Patrick.

THE REFORMATION AND AFTER

The Reformation was a total disaster in Ireland, and there are a number of reasons for this. When King Henry VIII decided to cast caution to the winds, England's writ travelled no further than the Pale. Efforts of his successors to impose the Reformation on Ireland were opposed by the old English Catholics or Anglo-Irish. They acknowledged the authority of the English monarch in temporal matters, but they did not acknowledge his spiritual power.

Nevertheless, efforts were made by the English monarchs to bring Ireland within the compass of the Crown. Penal laws and royal edicts emanated from England; how they were applied to the country depended on the authority and state of mind of the viceroy. One of these viceroys, the Marquess of Ormonde, tried to stamp out all traces of the Catholic Church, along with its congregation.

Queen Elizabeth I was not a religious bigot, but her purpose in trying to subdue Ireland was to obliterate the Irish race and to make the Gaels loyal subjects of the Crown.

Queen Anne, vigorously upholding the Protestant succession, believed that the Roman Catholic Church was an evil international conspiracy to bring about total papal domination.

The history of the Reformation as it affected Ireland has been written about at length; so have the Penal Laws. Close ties between priests and people in Ireland can be traced to the Reformation and the penal era. It is questionable whether the hierarchy could have survived in Ireland but for the continuing conspiracy on the part of the faithful to conceal their whereabouts. Laws which banished clergy from the land exacted stiff penalties for wrongdoers. Execution was certain in many cases for priests and bishops caught; large fines, if not death, for those who harboured them.

A dossier sent to Rome by Archbishop Walsh of Dublin in 1907 listed 292 causes which were felt to merit further investigation by the Congregation of Rites with a view to beatification. The list covers the period of martyrdom from 1572 to the close of Anne's reign in 1714, when executions ceased. Rome rejected eleven of the names on the list because of confused identity, and deferred another twenty-two due to the lack of evidence that death was principally inflicted because of the profession of faith. But this still left many Irish martyrs who may be said to have received Rome's approval while awaiting concrete evidence of sanctity. Most were priests and religious people, for it was against them that the law was enforced in its extremes.

The laity also had their martyrs. Under Elizabeth, for example, those executed were eight bishops, eighteen secular priests, forty-five religious and twenty-six lay people, including one woman. Many were hanged, some in mass executions like the fifty-three Dominicans of the Coleraine and Derry communities. Many wasted to death in the prisons. Two Trinitarians were drowned by Puritans while returning to Ireland from France. Others were killed by Cromwell's persecutions, which surpassed all others.

Ireland's first saint during this period, Oliver Plunkett, was canonized during the Holy Year celebrations in 1974–5. He was the last Roman Catholic to be martyred at Tyburn, London. He is an outstanding martyr of the penal era. He had a strong faith and a stubborn nature, with an acute sense of justice. He was born in County Meath in 1629, the son of a well-connected Anglo-Norman family related to the Earls of Fingall and Roscommon. He was educated by his uncle, the abbot of St Mary's Benedictine Abbey, Dublin. He went to the Irish College, Rome, and after ordination he stayed in Rome, where he took degrees in civil and canon law; he represented the Irish bishops and lectured at Propaganda College.

In 1669 O'Reilly, Archbishop of Armagh, died in France and Pope Clement IX appointed Plunkett to set about putting church affairs in order. As primate he called the Synod of Clones to see to the needs of the Church. This synod laid down rules for the discipline of the clergy. He engaged in controversy with Archbishop Talbot, and he intervened in a dispute between the Franciscans and Dominicans. This followed attempts by the Dominicans to re-establish themselves after the banishment law had been relaxed.

But the mounting tide renewed anti-Catholicism as it spread over the Irish Sea from England in 1673. There was everywhere a new drive against Roman Catholics. Mass was banned in Limerick and Cork; clergy were expelled from Galway. Late in 1673 an edict was issued from Dublin demanding that all clergy were to be out of the country by Christmas. Dr Plunkett went underground and ran his affairs in secret. The crunch came for him in 1677 when a letter to the English authorities from Brussels implicated him in a plot to cause a French invasion of Ireland and to restore the Catholic faith. He was discovered, arrested and imprisoned in Dublin Castle.

But at Dundalk the jury were unable to convict him. The Crown pressed ahead with new charges of fomenting a Catholic rebellion. Fearful that an Irish court might again acquit him, the authorities moved the proceedings to London. He was imprisoned at Newgate, which had housed many a martyr in its day. At the winter assizes the jury failed to indict him. Nevertheless he was tried the following summer. The anti-Catholic fever following the allegations in 1678 of a Catholic plot by Titus Oates mounted. The prosecution witnesses included one who later admitted perjury and two who were later hanged for robbery.

Plunkett was convicted of high treason and was hanged, drawn and quartered in 1681. The day after his death the Popish Plot was finally exposed as a fraud. Before his death he wrote to his nephew Michael Plunkett saying that he never sought to introduce the Catholic religion except by teaching and preaching. He was beatified by Pope Benedict XV on 23 May 1920. St Oliver has a strong following in Ireland and thousands flocked to see his head, which is preserved in St Peter's Church, Drogheda.

THE RE-AWAKENING

The Roman Catholic Church in Ireland emerged from the penal era spiritually rich but materially poor. It could never effectively identify with the poor, sunk as it was in dire poverty. The aim was for education, for without it there was no hope of arousing the people from their pitiful resignation. The Church was not able to act effectively in the rural areas, where small portions of land could not support all who required to be fed from it. Archbishop John McHale of Tuam criticized the authorities for their neglect, often to the discomfort of his fellow bishops who preferred more prudent approaches.

The controversy over government-sponsored national schools is long and complicated. These schools only affected a small portion of the people. The Church had to get involved. The Presentation Sisters were first in the field, and they were organized on a diocesan basis, with each house autonomous. In 1802 Edmund Ignatius Rice, a Waterford merchant, opened a school in the city for the education of the poor. That was the start of the congregation which perhaps more than any other was responsible for the swift advance of Irish education – the congregation of Christian brothers known as the Irish Christian Brothers. Edmund Rice was born at Callan,

County Kilkenny, in 1762, and he went to Waterford in 1778 to join his uncle, a successful merchant. He married in 1785, but his wife died four years later during a hunting expedition. The tragedy changed his life: he turned to the city's poor, and he decided that his future was to be taken up with providing for their educational needs.

In 1796 he and his friends sought permission from Rome to set up a society to provide for free education for poor boys. Their first school, called Mount Sion, was followed by others in rapid succession. By the time he had retired in 1838 there were twenty-two schools in Ireland and England.

The congregation adopted the rule of the Presentation Sisters, but that proved unsuitable because of the peculiar diocesan structure of the sisters. Pope Pius VII then gave permission for them to follow the rule of the De La Salle Brothers. These brothers were formed by those who desired to continue to follow the original rule.

AFTERWORD: MARY'S CHURCH

France has its Lourdes, Portugal its Fatima and Ireland its Knock. The Knock shrine, in County Mayo, is the most popular place of pilgrimage in Ireland; it draws a million souls a year. It was the scene of an apparition of the Virgin Mary. At Knock on 21 August 1879 Mary appeared to fifteen villagers at the gable of the parish church. She was accompanied by two other figures, one said to be St John the Baptist, the other St Joseph. On St John's left was a large altar and on it was a lamb facing towards the figures. Unlike Lourdes, no message was given. The apparition at Knock is still under investigation, but Rome has approved devotion to Our Lady of Knock. About 600 cures have been attributed to the intercession of the Virgin. It is not known why Mary chose Knock as a sacred site. The most popular explanation is that she appeared there to give reassurance during a difficult period in Ireland's history; the people's faith was being tested by poverty, overcrowding and enforced emigration.

SELECT BIBLIOGRAPHY

Edmund Curtis, *A History of Ireland* (Methuen).

I. J. Herring, *History of Ireland* (John Murray).

Jim Cantwell, *Holy Places of Ireland* (New English Library).

J. M. Flood, *Ireland: Its Saints and Scholars* (Talbot Press).

Michael Sheane, *Saint Patrick's Missionary Journeys In Ireland* (Arthur H. Stockwell).

Michael Sheane, *Ulster & St Patrick* (Highfield Press).

P. W. Joyce, *A Concise History of Ireland* (M. H. Gill & Son).

Rev. Ambrose Coleman, *Historical Memoirs of the City of Armagh* (Browne & Nolan).